Praise for *Art of the Conversation*

"Communication is an art form. How you have conversations affects your impact. Listen to Jonathan—soak in his wisdom and you will find that you have elevated your influence to the highest levels."

—Jeremie Kubicek, Visionary of GiANT and Wall Street Journal Best Seller, The 5 Voices, The Peace Index, and The Communication Code

"In *Art of the Conversation*, Jonathan skillfully illustrates the profound impact of conversations on our relationships, productivity, and overall well-being. By emphasizing the artistry inherent in conversations and the importance of active listening and intentional dialogue, this book offers a roadmap for leaders to truly connect with themselves and their teams. With practical guidance and insightful anecdotes, it equips leaders with invaluable tools to inspire, motivate, and lead with empathy and practicality. A must-read for anyone striving to cultivate authentic leadership and meaningful conversations in today's dynamic world."

—Steve Cockram, GiANT Co-Founder

"In a time of increasing polarization, *Art of the Conversation* emerges as a practical guide for people seeking to build common ground. With profound insights into the universal human desire for communication and respect, Jonathan lays groundwork for fostering genuine connections and nurturing inclusive communities through authentic conversations. This book is a timely reminder that meaningful dialogue has the power to bridge divides and cultivate unity."

—Dr. Nika White, DEIB & Leadership Consultant and author of Inclusion Uncomplicated published by Forbes Books

"*Art of the Conversation* is equal parts inspirational and practical. In a time when division is on the rise and connection is diminishing, this book provides a roadmap for creating common ground through meaningful and authentic communication. If you want to transform your relationships, improve your productivity, and create more spaces of belonging, this book is for you!"

—Dr. Jessica Sharp, Organizational Psychologist and Founder, Sharp Brain Consulting

"*Art of the Conversation* is a great reminder of the power of words... to help shape, engage, elevate, and if we are not careful... diminish. Artists tackle their work and the creation of masterpieces with great inspiration and intentionality, and our conversations deserve that same degree of care. The book has certainly made me rethink when, why, and how I speak, with a purview to edifying and encouraging all those with whom I am privileged to interact in business and life."

—G. T. "Toby" Stansell, CEO and Author

"Reading *Art of the Conversation* is like sitting with a dear friend and hearing and feeling deeply seen. Jonathan calls a spade a spade and he does it with a velvet hammer…smooth but forceful. His words paint a picture of something that everyone struggles with… using their communication to build others up rather than tear people down with 'reckless' communication styles. Gallup's research shows that only 34% of the working world is engaged at work. I wonder what would happen if the business community bought this book, had all their employees read it and then challenged them to apply the contents? It would accelerate revenue, create engagement and make people better human beings. I plan to use his book when working with teams and I believe that the contents will still be applicable many years from now. Read this book and challenge yourself today to sharpen your 'vocal art.'"

—Traci Newkirk, Entrepreneur and Business Coach, Human Potential Advisors

ART of the CONVERSATION

by Jonathan R. Parker

Copyright © 2024 by Jonathan R. Parker, all rights reserved.

First Edition

Printed in the United States of America

ISBN 9798333145505

Cover photo by Halim Karya Art
Cover and book design by Wendy Willard

For information about special discounts for bulk purchases or for booking the author for an event, please visit thejonathanrparker.com.

Contents

Introduction
The Duo of Universal Needs 1

Chapter One
You, the Artist 9

Chapter Two
Curiosity as Your Canvas 17

Chapter Three
Underpainting with Questions 29

Chapter Four
The Brushstrokes of Listening 39

Chapter Five
Sharing Your Colors 51

Chapter Six
Your Studio, Your Legacy 63

Reference
Vocal Art Key Takeaways 71

A Time for Gratitude 74

About the Author 77

To the One Who Answered Well

XLI-XII-XXVIII

INTRODUCTION
The Duo of Universal Needs

When I was young, I had seizures so serious that I did not talk until I was almost five years old. I grunted through most of my toddler years. Literally. My mom understood me, as only moms can; but the communication delays caused other delays. I failed the first grade because I could not effectively communicate.

Now I talk for a living.

I know. The irony is not lost on me. When my mom hears that I am speaking publicly, she chuckles to herself and even gets a bit teary-eyed. I am not supposed to be the guy communicating to rooms full of people. Compared to my challenging communicative start, it is like seeing a fish thrive on land or a dog walking on two legs. I should not be able to do this, much less be an expert on conversation and effective communication.

But once my talking got going, I started running my mouth and never really stopped. In sixth grade, I gave a speech that drew immense applause; and from there I was hooked on the idea of public speaking. It was not until years later, when all grown up and working my adult job, that my perspective on communication made a major shift. The realization was "pointed out to me" that in the process of all my talking, I had failed to adequately develop my skills as a listener. A challenge was issued: no speaking for six months. Sit and listen. Challenge accepted. Six months later, my outlook on communication had been transformed. I was more attuned to those around me; and as time went on, people seemed more inclined to talk to me. The experience piqued my curiosity and I wanted to learn everything I could about conversations. As I reflected on those muted months, the difference in how I engaged with people exposed some simple, yet profound, universal truths. I began to notice two desires that all human beings share, and recognition of these two human desires brought both personal and professional change in my approach to communication.

I start most of my talks on the subject of conversation with the same question:

"What do you believe are the deepest desires that people hold?"

Do not overthink the question. Just generally, think about the average person walking around. At the core, what does this person desire most? What drives that person? At this point in my life, I have asked this question countless times; and essentially I get the same answers every time. The most common answers

I receive are happiness, love, fame, wealth, belonging, relationship, and significance. These are all great things that people value and work towards, but not necessarily desires that people universally share.

So what are these common human desires? Over the years, I have seen that every person no matter age, gender, race, nationality, socioeconomic status—insert whatever descriptor here—every person desires the opportunity to communicate and the respect to be heard.

Let me say that again: All human beings desire the opportunity to communicate and the respect to be heard.

> * *Use these wide margins and the blank pages between chapters for notes, brainstorms, or doodles along the journey.*

I have three boys under the age of ten (Yes, my wife is indeed a saint). All my youngest child wants in the world is to have the opportunity to communicate. He desires it so much that he will scream until I give him the respect to listen. My ninety-year-old grandmother was somewhat slower and much more soft spoken than my son, but all she wanted was the opportunity to communicate. She wanted her children, grandchildren, and great-grandchildren to give her the respect to be heard. This core desire applies in any circle: families, coworkers, social circles, religious parishioners, high schoolers. The list goes on and on. Every person is looking for the opportunity to communicate and for the respect to be heard when speaking.

When we recognize these two universal desires, our engagement with others carries the potential to create something unique. Our words are like paint. We create what I call "vocal art." Unfortunately, most of us communicate like a reckless artist. Instead of using our words intentionally, we throw them at a canvas and hope that when it is all over the finished art will somehow look beautiful. That approach creates bad vocal art, and unfortunately we have become accustomed to accepting it as such. Have you ever heard the comments, "Oh! Well, you just didn't understand what I was saying," or "That's not what I meant; you just interpreted it wrong," or even, "I'm just not any good at talking to people"? Why are these comments made? They are made because people speak as lazy vocal artists, rejecting the notion that quality conversation actually derives from skills that can be honed. Consequently, we approach our human interactions with very little confidence and set our bar for great conversation severely low.

We see this low bar not only in our personal relationships but also in our communities. Conversation is critical in fostering true community because it allows us to share mutual ideas, stories, and experiences around a specific topic. Within these encounters we develop common ground, the space/room you have in a relationship to disagree with someone without losing the relationship and/or disengaging from the conversation.

It is easier to have broad space in which to move when we agree, but genuine relationships are built when we can agree *and* also disagree without forfeiting the relationship. Common ground is the by-product of good conversations and is the foundation necessary for us to talk about the hard stuff.

My goal is to empower you to create remarkable vocal art by providing practical steps to hone your conversational craft. You can be known and remembered for your ability to make great conversation. You can learn how to express yourself more clearly, to dig deeper in relationships, and to increase your productivity. Your legacy can be one of an individual who recognized these common human desires for communication and respect, created space for these engagements to occur, and allowed others the chance to be heard.

In today's crazy world, most days feel as if there is more division and less communication than at any other point in my lifetime. Now is a time where we need to find common ground more than ever. Today's world makes some people feel hopeless, but what I see is opportunity. I am still naive enough to think we can change the world. We can change the status quo. We can change the trajectory of our communities and embrace the richness and beauty that human interaction creates.

How will we do this? One conversation at a time. One blank canvas, full of possibilities. Are you in? Then let us embark on a journey together!

Big Takeaways & Next Steps

CHAPTER ONE
You, the Artist

Conversations are your vocal art. *You are an artist.* If you consider yourself a creative type, you might readily agree. If you do not consider yourself creative, the "artist" label may feel like more of a stretch. Perhaps a very big stretch depending on your perceived skill level. You may even be tempted to argue—but follow me here.

All people are artists in the sense that the conversations we create have vocal art. Every time we speak, we are creating and displaying art. It is not just something we do; vocal art is weaved into our identities. Through words, as well as silence, we build invisible masterpieces of thought, imagery, and emotion that invade a visible world in ways no picture could even hope to capture. Sounds too intense? It should, because it is. Words hold a tremendous amount of power.

Why are the stories we read in books almost always better than watching the same plots unfold in movies? Words paint pictures that simply cannot be captured in the same way by physical means. And these pictures are unique to each individual.

Every day, you and I make art with our words; and in the same way that a painting is a reflection of the painter, your conversations are a reflection of you. They are your distinctive vocal art.

This way of thinking challenges the status quo of the fast-paced, digital world in which we find ourselves. Sadly, our current culture seems to have lost the art of how to have good, meaningful conversations. We did not value them for so long that, at best, they are like a hazy memory. The same thing happened with dancing. How many people do you know who truly can tango or waltz? Something that was once valued and part of culture has become minimal at best. I see the same thing happening with conversation, and I am on a mission to stop that trajectory.

Most of us are reckless with our words and stingy with our listening. We start and stop talking without much thought or intention. We are reckless artists— haphazardly throwing paint against a canvas without any regard for the end result. (And yes, even abstract artists utilize their paint with intention.)

Kevin Stacey of TrainRight, Inc. once told me that around 60,000 thoughts go through our brains every single day. For a majority of people, 40,000 of those thoughts are negative. In essence, for every one positive thought a person has, two negative ones are waiting to drown it out. We are underdogs in a battle we did not even know we were fighting. Ultimately, this kind of internal diatribe can alter our perception of reality. It does not matter how factually good I am at my job when 40,000 thoughts are telling me I am bad at it.

If a daily thought life is full of this ugly self-talk, how can one expect to create beautiful vocal art when talking to others?

The name of the game is giving the 20,000 positive thoughts priority over the negative—both in our own lives and in the lives of the people around us. Every person in our circle already has enough criticism going on between the ears: what went wrong, what detail was missed, what thing could have been done differently. That is why it is so important that we enter every conversation with the finesse and care of an artist. People need more positivity! Not in a cliche way but in a desperate one, and we have the power to help shift that inner monologue.

Use these wide margins and the blank pages between chapters for notes, brainstorms, or doodles along the journey.

The title for this book is very intentionally chosen. This book is a simultaneous focus on art and conversation—never one without the other.

Identifying as an artist conveys two things: who you are and what you create. Every single time you open your mouth to speak, you are creating art. Your speaking not only captures the subject but also reflects you as the vocal artist. My goal is to help you see yourself as an aspiring vocal artist and then give you everything you need to be a great conversationalist. But that is not the end; it is the launching pad. When you improve your conversation skills, you also improve your productivity, your relationship skills, and the depths of those relationships.

Have you heard the old adage, "What's remembered in song is remembered long?" It stands true because our brains are programmed to remember art. Maybe you do not remember a podcast you listened to a week ago, but you remember all the words to the song you heard after your first real break-up. Art makes us feel things so that we remember it.

The same thing is true of our conversations. I may not remember all the specifics, but I know when I have had a great conversation because of how it made me feel. The alternative is also true. I might forget the details of a fight, but I know for certain that I felt angry. In the same way, whether it is good or bad, art always leaves an impression. That is one reason why it is so challenging to truly mend broken relationships. Forgiveness might be granted in a moment but trust takes years to rebuild. The parties involved can still see the bad art and remember how it made them feel.

So the question remains: Are you wanting to be intentional with your art? Are you going to own your identity as an artist and start creating beautiful vocal art that leaves a legacy of which you can be proud? Or, are you going to be passive and reckless thereby leaving a collection of ugly art in your wake?

The choice is yours. (Ahem… a piece of advice: Pick option one!)

==This manuscript is your handbook. Write in it, highlight within it, dog ear the pages. It is your guide to becoming a great vocal artist.== ✱

So let us proceed toward making great art. Allow me to introduce you to your canvas.

Big Takeaways & Next Steps

CHAPTER TWO
Curiosity as Your Canvas

Say what you will about cliches, but there is a reason they gain such renown. For the most part, there are grains of truth in them that can be valuable. "Curiosity killed the cat" might be the most damaging cliche to ever gain repute. I am a dog guy, so I am not so bothered about the cat. However, I do care that the cat gave curiosity such a bad rap. What if the cat did not die? What if it learned something? Sure, maybe it fell, looked foolish, or was wounded; but death is rather extreme. What if the cat actually got stronger or its life became richer in some way?

In all seriousness, curiosity is becoming a lost art. In the last few decades, our society has vastly undervalued curiosity. Think about it. Limiting curiosity as much as possible has been a technique used by people every day, and unfortunately most of the time it is with children. No shame. I know how mind-numbingly maddening determined toddlers can be; but when you think about it, they are just showing us their curiosity about the world around them. For decades our entire school systems were set up to minimize curiosity as much as possible. The typical process was built on a culture of "sit down, stay quiet, and regurgitate information when asked." This has produced the rise of project-based learning, schooling at home, and renewed focus within traditional schools to push students toward being curious. Yet we still have a long way to go.

Just a few decades back, wanting to learn something new involved going to the library to use an encyclopedia or to read a book on the topic. When my dad had a plumbing issue at our house, he picked up the phone to call a plumber. Crazy, right?! And even crazier, people actually enjoyed asking for help from an expert. This was even expected. Can you imagine that? Time was deliberately set aside for asking and answering questions. A plumber did not get in trouble for spending an hour talking with someone to help the customer navigate an issue because this communication was part of the job. It was a communal pleasure to exchange knowledge and to lock eyes while talking and listening. People had the opportunity to communicate *and* to be heard... regularly.

Fast forward to today. If we want to know something, we "Google" it. This happens *so* often that the search engine Google, once a noun, has become a verb. When "how to" instructions are needed, Google connects us to our good friend YouTube, totally eliminating the need for any actual human interaction.

Curiosity does not get practiced.

Do not get me wrong: technology is awesome and is a gift in so many ways. However, it has all but ruined our ability to be curious alongside each other. The opportunity to regularly practice curiosity among the community has vanished; in its place is another opportunity to be isolated and buried in our phones.

My wife gives me a hard time because I do not know how to do more things around the house. Sure, I could stand to be a little more proficient; but truthfully, I like having the excuse to call my handy friends to have a conversation. I like getting to ask questions and then listening as they share their expertise. I like being an amateur and fumbling through learning something new. Is this the most efficient? No. But it is human, and I will take that approach any day.

Conversation is the most natural and unnatural thing we do. Our current culture has made conversation weird, awkward, and uncomfortable. We have been denied, almost robbed, of the opportunity to be curious. Ask too many questions and you are annoying. People find curiosity off putting and weird.

"I don't know, man. Why don't you just Google it?!"

"Well, yes, thank you. I am aware that is an option, but I would actually like *your* input."

Society is annoyed by the curious. Is it the time investment that the process of discovery demands? Are we afraid of looking dumb or of being exposed in some way? What is the worst that could happen: I might fail or look stupid? So what! I had the chance to learn and to get better.

Quick side note to parents: Try not to be annoyed at your kids if they ask something out of curiosity. There is so much they do not know and they look at us as super humans. Of course they are going to ask us all the questions. We will not bat one thousand here; no one does. However, dismissing their questions or shutting them down communicates that our kids should not be curious.

Supervisors, if an employee comes to ask for clarity about work or to discuss an office issue and is met with dismissal, you are creating a culture where curiosity is not valued. When curiosity is not celebrated, it will not be replicated. It will be squelched and eventually die out, which is bad news for any company.

✱ Without curiosity, there can be no creativity; and that is the worst place any organization can find itself.

If you have not been cultivating curiosity, do not be too hard on yourself. Our culture has taught us to be that way. The media does not want us to be curious, but would rather have us siloed and complacent, suggesting we choose our news sources based on our political party or political ideas. This is terrible advice. Trapped in our little bubbles, we will not grow or think analytically. We will simply confirm our biases and allow our empathetic muscles to atrophy. The last time I checked, complacency never changed anything. Blind compliance certainly never made anything better. As Bernard Baruch famously said, "Millions saw the apple fall and Newton was the one who asked why."

At this point, you might be thinking, "Okay, Jonathan. We get it. Curiosity will not kill anybody, and is actually somewhat important." Wonderful! Now, I want you to understand *how* truly important it is.

==Curiosity is the canvas for all of your vocal art; it is the foundation.== ✱

Good conversations don't exist in the absence of curiosity, and we will never have a decent conversation with someone about something we aren't curious about. At the same time, without that element of curiosity, we will be looking for an exit when we sense we are in a conversation with someone who is not the least bit curious about us. Have you ever tried painting without a canvas? You would have a guaranteed mess on your hands.

When you and I stop being curious, we become familiar. And what does familiarity breed? The answer is in another cliché: familiarity breeds contempt. Yet, I do not fully agree with that. The word contempt feels too angry, and we might be tempted to dismiss the idea outright. If I can use a different shade here, more accurately I would say familiarity breeds complacency.

With one question, I can tell if a spouse or partner has become complacent in a relationship: "What are you getting your significant other for Christmas?"

If that question is met with a dumbfounded look, do you know what that tells me? After 364 days, that other person has become familiar.

We need curiosity to run parallel with familiarity. Flip the whole thing on its head. The more familiar we are with someone, the more curious we should be about them. The more familiar we are with our job, the more curious we should be about it. In light of what we know, what we have done, and what we have tried, what can we still experience differently? What is another way to look at it?

But where do we begin? I am so glad you asked. First, take a few minutes to make a list of the people you know the best. These would be your ride or die people—the ones you know better than anyone else.

Once you have your list, take a moment to think of something each of those people do not already know about you. More than likely, something specific came to mind right away. That is the thought you should share. Resist the temptation to jump down to the third or fourth thing that they do not know about you. Do not allow your internal dialogue to talk you down. Now, here's the homework. Get in touch with those people you listed to tell them the first thing that came to your mind.

In our closest relationships, it is easy to believe that we already know everything there is to know about each other. We must actively combat that lie by embracing the awkwardness to dig deeper in order to be vulnerable with our people. That is where the richness of true relationships lies.

Most of the time, when I consult with companies, it is because HR brought me in. Human Resources people tend to see the value in staff actually talking and listening to each other. Go figure.

One time, I met two people who had known each other for twenty years. They had worked alongside each other in HR at the same company, raised kids alongside each other, coached sports together, and generally spent a great deal of time together. When they did the exercise I outlined above, they found out for the first time that each of them had been adopted. It immediately took their friendship to another level. Their relationship was never bad, but it became so much richer in a moment of transparency.

I try to keep this principle in mind every time I take my wife on a date. Theoretically, she is the person I should know the best in the entire world; but instead of being content to become familiar, I have made it a discipline to choose curiosity. I ask her to share something with me that I did not already know about her week or something that happened in her childhood.

Thinking we know all there is to know about someone is a dangerous place to be. When we fall for that lie, we stop being curious. We stop asking questions. It is the norm that we must learn to resist. We must keep practicing curiosity to grow in it. We must keep it at the forefront of our minds because we are swimming upstream. Reclaiming curiosity means rejecting complacency and refusing compliance; neither of those are passive things.

In order to take hold of something, we need to know what it is and what it is not. Let us mark out the dimensions of curiosity—where does our canvas begin and end?

Curiosity is not compromising our convictions and it doesn't have to mean conflict.

Curiosity does not require a change in who we are or what we value. Asking questions, wanting to learn, and even the desire to make an informed decision does not necessitate changing our convictions. Yet, most corporate organizations are terrified of their employees being on LinkedIn. There is a fear that seeing the available options will make those employees question or compare their current jobs. (And, honestly, maybe it should.) Political parties do not want us to research all sides of an issue. Even religious groups get uncomfortable when someone decides to really dig in to study. It is time we learned that it is not compromising to investigate our position or beliefs. Curiosity grants us permission to explore opposing beliefs without undermining our own. When paired with healthy mental boundaries, curiosity is able to hold the tension between various ideas and opinions —without demanding concessions from the listener.

Curiosity does not equal complaining.

Sometimes people use their questions as a means to whine or to be passive aggressive, using a question to find the other people who will listen to gripes or enable self-pity. "Don't you think that _____ is just ridiculous?! Wouldn't you feel _____ if _____ had been done to you too?" Shared offense can certainly bond people together, but not in a healthy way. In many ways, engagement on that level is evidence of immaturity. This type of "misery loves company" should not be confused with the curiosity goals we are discussing here and is not the kind of communication we want to foster.

None of the things listed above are curiosity; and when we confuse them, we are left with a bad canvas. No matter how good an artist you might be, you will not be able to produce great art with a busted canvas. We need to be sure the canvas is clean, free of dust, and pure. If not, we will never produce our best art.

Now for the better path.
Here is what curiosity actually is.

True curiosity is courageous.

In a world that is made of "fake it until you make it," people try to be experts at everything. The courageous steps out and says, "I don't know. Would you help me?" In a culture of Googling and figuring it out ourselves, it is brave to actually ask another human being a question. We reach out to others because we believe they have knowledge, experience, or insight to offer. We engage in a courageous act by admitting to someone that we do not know.

True curiosity produces connection.

When a person shares something with me that I did not know before, I become more connected to that individual. The same is true of the inverse. When I share something with a person that was not known about me, we become more connected.

True curiosity is contagious.

People start seeing the fruit of curiosity and they want it, too. One person being curious spreads the desire for curiosity and lays the foundation—creates the canvas—for great conversation.

Einstein said, "I have no special talents. I am only passionately curious."

Now that we've got a canvas, it is time to paint.

Big Takeaways & Next Steps

CHAPTER THREE
Underpainting with Questions

In painting, the first layer of paint that serves as the base for all the other layers is called the underpainting. The underpainting lays the groundwork for the entire picture since it is the layer upon which all the colors will be built. As we create our vocal artwork, the questions we ask serve as our underpainting.

Questions are instrumental, and this would be great news if asking good questions was an easy task. Unfortunately, it can feel like the opposite because asking good questions can be a challenge. Good questions take some forethought, and that is exactly why many of us will not ask good questions. We make excuses due to the difficulty and settle for surface level conversations. Over time, the end result is that we are willing to accept shallow relationships that allow us to continue concealing our fears and insecurities.

Consequently, we walk through life painting unimpressive, forgettable vocal art.

Telling, on the other hand, feels pleasing to us. Telling allows me to reveal what I know instead of asking questions to reveal what I do not know. When we do not know things, we can feel ignorant and ashamed. Rather than being vulnerable by asking questions, we hide our ignorance and cling to our pride. (Ouch… that stings a little, does it not?)

Listening around us, we hear many people who model talking and telling very well but not asking. Even if someone seems to be asking questions, listening more closely will reveal that most of the questions are simply statements with the wrong punctuation. How many times have you heard the following: "You know that cannot be true, right?," "You have no idea where you are going, huh?," or, my favorite, "You were done, right?" Ever wonder why the people on our TV screens are called "talking heads?" They are not called asking heads, curious heads, or inquisitive heads. They just talk and talk; and if they do happen to take a moment to actually ask a question, they are quick to interrupt as soon as the guest starts answering.

Genuinely asking questions means actively listening; however, in all honesty, most of us do not want to commit to doing that. ★ Asking questions requires surrendering control of a conversation. At that point in the conversation, the other person tells us the information and when the conversation is done. This is what the majority of people struggle with the most when it comes to asking questions: giving up control of the conversation.

Asking good questions is hard, but I have got good news. We are one hundred percent capable of doing hard things.

Perhaps, in the past, your questions have received only shallow answers. Therefore, you may be thinking, "Okay, Jonathan. I understand that my questions are important, but what if people are not giving me answers I can use?" Maybe we get bad answers because we are asking bad questions. Instead of prepping our curiosity canvas with a welcoming, open sky blue, we chose a dark, black background but then wonder why the puffy white clouds and sunshine seem out of place. If the first paints we put on our canvas are incredibly restrictive, it is hard to recover after that. Initiating a conversation is the same way. If we start poorly, we are setting the course on a bad trajectory. If we paint arbitrary, reckless strokes, it does not set us up for success. The good news is that we can do better.

Becoming a good question asker takes some mental work and preparation. We will need to brainstorm good questions and then practice asking them, instead of hoping to stumble into effective conversation.

Once we have internally prepared to ask questions, we must be willing to persevere. There is a psychological piece involved: sticking to the conversation even if we do not see immediate results. For example, if you have only $12 in your account, it is difficult to spend $10. If you have been operating with a conversational deficit, you will need some time to build up your confidence and establish new habits. You must keep creating new questions, asking them, and maintaining the right mindset to keep those questions going. You need to believe this process is worth it and understand the benefit these new insights will bring.

Finally, I suggest that you be prayerful, mindful, or meditative about the questions. Haphazardly throwing out rhetorical, aggressive questions has the potential to hurt people. Most of us would not deliberately set out to do harm; we would prefer to be better at asking questions if we only knew where to start.

Thankfully, in my years of studying what makes conversations meaningful, I have learned many helpful techniques to keep in mind as my canvas is prepared with conscientious questions. If you are willing to try, the following are some practical techniques for how to start.

UNDERPAINTING TECHNIQUE #1
Ask what or how questions rather than why questions

I will start this technique with a quick caveat. Philosophically, you should always know your why. There is power in knowing why you do what you do. Having a clear why gives a vision for the present and the future.

Relational conversations, however, are different. As a general rule, avoid asking why questions because they can put people on the defensive. Consider how you feel when someone asks, "Why didn't you text me back?" More than likely, you feel either a little put off or accused of something. This would be similar to boxing: one is throwing jabs while the other blocks.

What and how questions, on the other hand, are disarming and invite someone to share a relational story ✱ rather than a philosophical explanation. For example, we could reframe the earlier question by asking, "How is your day going? I sent you a text but didn't hear back, so I wanted to be sure you were okay." Swapping out a few words allows us to ask the same question without implicating the other party.

Now, there are also times when we find ourselves on the defensive side because of a why question. In this situation, we can mentally rephrase the why question and repeat it back to the person. "What I am hearing you ask is what happened that led to me missing your text. Is that what you are asking?" Reframing the question in this way de-escalates the conversation and takes both parties out of the boxing ring.

UNDERPAINTING TECHNIQUE #2
Ask a follow-up question before making a statement

Most people do not fully communicate everything they are trying to say the first time they say it. Follow-up questions demonstrate that we have been listening and also confirm that we have accurately understood what was communicated. Within that initial interaction, we are already able to give someone the opportunity to communicate and the respect to be heard. From there, any statement we make will carry more weight because of the established connection early on.

Once a connection is made, try not to be the reason the conversation dies unless you physically have to leave. Every conversation has to come to an end, but it does not have to end prematurely on your watch.

Maybe this type of situation sounds familiar: you are in a conversation with someone, neither asks a question, and both are just standing there awkwardly. In this situation, short strokes were used that did not come together to create anything. The remedy is to listen intently and then ask a good follow-up question based on what you heard.

UNDERPAINTING TECHNIQUE #3
Ask for an invitation before giving your opinion

Today's culture has the belief that just because people are talking to us, they want our opinions. We know that we do not always want the opinions of others; but interestingly, we assume they must want ours. Bombarding people with our opinions is like breaking into their houses, plopping down on couches, kicking our feet up on the coffee tables, and asking them to bring us a glass of water. We were never invited, much less offered refreshments. People are much more open to receiving when they have extended an invitation, just as they would be much more likely to invite us in after we have knocked at doors and waited for them to answer.

If we have thoughts to share, we can say something such as, "Hey, are you open to some feedback on that?," "I have some thoughts. Would you like my opinion?," or "Can I offer a different perspective on that?" Letting someone know we have been listening and have thoughts on what was said will spark curiosity. More than likely, the person will be open to hearing our feedback, instead of it feeling forced upon them.

UNDERPAINTING TECHNIQUE #4
Understand the relationship

When asking questions, it is also important that we understand the social relationship: is it with a co-worker, a peer to peer, or superior to subordinate? Whatever it is, we must consider the relationship before asking the question. There may be power dynamics in play that will alter the way we proceed. There is also the consideration of the duration and the common ground of the relationship because those factors determine what questions can be asked and how they should be asked. In some cases, we can ask bigger, more poignant questions; in others, those questions would not be appropriate.

Lighting a bonfire is approached in an entirely different way than lighting a candle on a birthday cake. How I handle each lighting determines if the fire will be beneficial or harmful—if it will either achieve the goal or create a potential problem.

My best friend was my boss for ten years. At the start of any conversation, we would say, "Okay, I'm wearing the friend hat right now," or "Hey, it is the boss hat for the next thirty minutes." In situations where several relationships are at play, it is our responsibility to know what relational conversation we are having. Then, we can set the context and expectation so that the other person knows which social relationship is talking.

UNDERPAINTING TECHNIQUE #5
Consider the context

If you are making a bonfire, you want it to last for more than thirty seconds; but if you are dealing with a birthday candle, thirty seconds is sufficient. All it has to do is last through one rendition of "Happy Birthday." Before lighting either the bonfire or the candle, you must consider the logistics.

The same is true with asking good questions: keep the context in mind. Is it the right time and place to ask the question? If not, when would be a good time? Where should I ask it, and what tone does it require? The question you want to ask might be appropriate to ask—but not in front of a crowd. On the other hand, it might be appropriate and the most efficient to ask in the open office so that everyone can have clarity.

Does this sound like quite a bit of prep work? Perhaps. Practically, it is more about slowing down and thinking intentionally. If you want to be a great vocal artist, you will need some preparation to hone your craft in order to prep your canvas with the most appropriate underpainting questions. You want to use questions to grow common ground. A fire can provide something for yourself and others to gather around or it can burn everything to the ground. A bonfire is awesome. A wildfire? Not so much.

Big Takeaways & Next Steps

CHAPTER FOUR
The Brushstrokes of Listening

When I am teaching The Art of the Conversation to corporate groups, I use a go-to exercise to kick off the section about the brushstrokes of listening.

Picture this or, better yet, try it out on your own. To start I ask everyone to line up shoulder-to-shoulder, chronologically according to birth month. January birthdays start at the left and then proceed down the line to December. From there, I tell the participants to close their eyes and put their hands up, palms facing out. Then, I pause for a minute to let everyone feel sort of weird, nervous, and vulnerable. It is great! After that comes the interesting part of the exercise. With their hands up and eyes closed, I ask them to get in reverse order—starting with December on the left going all the way down the line to January.

You can probably guess what happens next. Almost everyone immediately starts talking while the true introverts in the room wince a little bit and close their eyes a little tighter as they wait for the exercise to be over. Perhaps you have heard the saying, "Too many cooks in the kitchen." I observe it in real time every time I conduct this exercise.

One time when I did this, the group needed twenty minutes for fourteen people to invert their birthdays. Why? Everyone started talking over each other, instead of taking a moment to actually listen. How many people needed to talk to complete this exercise? Maybe one or two. How many people started talking? All of them.

So far in our journey toward creating great vocal art, we have talked about our canvas and about our canvas preparation. Now we begin adding layers. For the next two components of our vocal art, we will discuss brushstrokes of listening and sharing of colors. For these elements, we will talk in two main categories—obstacles and opportunities.

Listening is one of the hardest paints to use. For most of us, it is significantly more difficult than talking because it does not come as naturally. ✳ Listening requires more mental work to stay engaged and takes more restraint to keep our mouths shut. As someone who talks for a living, I find I am always tired after teaching because I have run my mouth for hours; but in most cases, the audience is significantly more tired since the audience members had to listen for hours. As a general rule, we do not listen with the intent to understand. Oftentimes, we simply listen enough to know how we are going to respond—waiting (somewhat) patiently for our turn to talk again. Our culture is full of passive listeners and active responders.

This brings us to the biggest obstacle to listening that most be overcome. To be good listeners, we must conquer our own perceptions. Setting aside perceptions to truly listen can be difficult. People tend to act based on what they perceive, instead of allowing things to play out. They may have an idea of what might happen but will not know for sure unless they genuinely listen. There are three common obstacles that inhibit listening from happening.

LISTENING OBSTACLE #1
Perceived understanding—"I already know that"

We have all heard it before. We are mid-sentence when we hear, "Oh yeah, yeah... I know exactly what you mean." It is a phrase that runs rampant through bad vocal art. And we can all agree that no one likes hearing that phrase while we are still trying to talk! The problem is that if we do not actively listen to someone it is impossible for us to know for certain all that will be said. In addition, we are not inclined to listen when we believe we already understand.

Our minds tell us we already know the information; therefore, we tune out. During conversations, I regularly tell my brain to be quiet so that I can listen. Newsflash: We do not actually know everything. We may have an idea, but will not know for sure until we ✱ listen.

LISTENING OBSTACLE #2
Perceived outcomes—"I already know what will happen"

Imagine there is a party happening this weekend. You were invited but decided to decline. Maybe you had other obligations or maybe you just were not interested. Whatever the reason, you are not going. Later, a friend of yours comes to talk to you, chattering about how excited he is to go to the party. The moment you realize he wants to talk about the party, you decide to tune out. Not because you are mean. Probably not even intentionally. But, you know you are not going to the party; therefore, you assume that the conversation does not have much to do with you anyway. Why listen?

Fair? Not really. In this situation, we reveal that we care more about ourselves and our relationship to the party than the person who is communicating excitement about going. Good listeners are present and do not allow their own experiences to overshadow the experience of others.

LISTENING OBSTACLE #3
Perceived reaction—"I already know what I will feel, and I will not like it"

Sometimes we do not listen because we want to remain uninvolved. Ever heard the expression *blissfully unaware*? Some of us prefer to stay detached—passively aloof—because we do not want to deal with emotions we think we will face if we listen. Perhaps truly listening may require us to act on something we are not ready to face. It is more comfortable to tune out the other person so that we may hold on to our "plausible deniability." We do not want to listen to our partner say some hard things because we are not ready to apologize. We hear about a friend's job loss, but hope we do not bump into the person to hear it firsthand. Most of the time, people do not actually need that much from us. They want to feel our empathy, but we do not give them the opportunity because we assume it is going to require much more of us.

These obstacles stand in the way of our openness and ability to listen to others. They create barriers to building common ground and to painting beautiful vocal art. Instead, imagine if we could reframe (pun intended) these obstacles, drop the misconceptions that prevent us from connecting, and instead pick up better tools to create our art.

What we need are opportunities—better brushstrokes that empower us to listen and listen well. These are the listening tools that we need in order to paint well.

LISTENING OPPORTUNITY #1
Give undivided attention

At one point or another, you have probably been told you have to set yourself up to win. That is certainly the case with listening. In today's world, we are more accessible and also more distracted than ever. Everyday life naturally has lots of noise, so we need to be disciplined in creating the right environment to listen. That means we must consciously decide to tune in and then tune out distractions as much as possible.

Here is an example: You are meeting a friend to talk about some challenges he is facing in his marriage. Do not meet at a sports bar. Sports are awesome, and you and your friend really enjoy them. Unfortunately, the setting does not suit the conversation. The environment has TVs all over, allowing a million things to vie for attention, and people are expected to be loud. Just describing the atmosphere already confirms that the environment is not conducive to locking in and listening.

In addition to environmental factors, we must deal with potential distractions that are within our control. We should put our phones away and turn down music. Meeting in an office? If it's appropriate, close the door or put a sign on the door so people know not to interrupt. Making periodic eye contact with the person shows our focus is on them instead of what is happening around us. Some distractions are obvious and some are more covert; therefore, we can do the work to handle the ones we can identify.

Finally, we must be in the proper posture to listen, figuratively and literally. Physical posture communicates if we are listening or not. Slouched in a chair and leaning back with our arms crossed does not instill confidence that we care at all about what is being said. On the other hand, sitting up and leaning forward sends a much clearer signal that we are actually taking an interest in the other person and in the conversation. Our physical posture and our mental posture of committing to focus and of eliminating distractions work together to help us be great listeners.

LISTENING OPPORTUNITY #2
Listen for perspective before giving your perception

Perception is the view in; perspective is the view out. Each of us have opinions, and most of them are informed by individual perspectives. This is not an earth-shattering claim. Much of what we believe about the world is based on what we personally experience. With that in mind, it is important to remember that no one can have a "wrong" opinion since it is a personal opinion. So when we are listening, we should do our best to hear out a person no matter what our individual opinion might be. Make space to hear the other point of view.

Word from the wise: much time, energy, and hurt can be saved by hearing someone's perspective and then waiting to offer our perception until it is actually solicited.

Many times, people want to hear and value our perceptions. That is why they decide to share something with us in the first place. However, it is likely they did not want to have our perceptions forced on them.

Remember that candidly sharing our perspectives and perceptions can be intimidating, challenging, or painful. Those pains can be growing pains if we channel them properly—employing patience and waiting for an invitation to share. By doing so, we can establish more common ground.

LISTENING OPPORTUNITY #3
Show empathy

As you listen, take steps to connect with the person talking. Your listening will be demonstrated by asking follow-up questions to gain even more understanding.

Then, be vulnerable. Let the person know if you have had a similar experience. If you have not had a similar experience, you can certainly convey a level of empathy.

Vulnerability is a paradox. People assume others will perceive vulnerability as a weakness when the exact opposite is true. Studies conducted by Brené Brown found in her published writings show people respect and feel more connected with people who are willing to be vulnerable, causing vulnerability to be seen as strength. Brown has already done some beautiful work in this area, and I highly recommend researching her books for yourself.

✱ ==Empathy is a natural byproduct of true listening.== It is feeling *with* people—not just *for* them. It is connecting, and our world needs more of that.

LISTENING OPPORTUNITY #4
Use candor; embrace boundaries

Be honest at the onset of a conversation if your time or attention is going to be limited. It can be as simple as a few quick sentences: "I want to listen to you and give you my full attention, but I must tell you that I am waiting for a phone call," or "I would love to hear what you have to say, but I have ten minutes before my next meeting. Would that be enough time or should we schedule something later this week?"

People feel respected and valued when you are willing to be honest with them. Being vague does not help anyone. ✻

Setting healthy personal boundaries can be incredibly beneficial. Many think that putting time limits on a conversation, as described above, comes across as uncaring. Yet, how many times have we tuned out people because we genuinely did not have the emotional bandwidth or the time to give, but did not vocalize it? I would venture to guess the interaction was not positive in the long run, perhaps even leaving you feeling resentful or exhausted? An unwillingness to be candid about our personal boundaries—especially when dealing with available time, emotions, or otherwise—will ultimately lead to burnout and a much greater chance of tuning out and turning away from these common ground opportunities. Being open and honest is neither harsh nor unkind. Beginning our conversations in an honest way means that people will have a much better idea of where we stand, creating a safe space for the both of us.

Take some time to consider to whom you need to start listening again. Who have you tuned out or dismissed? Are there areas of your life where you overextended yourself and now need to practice a little candor by employing some better boundaries so you can be fully present?

With listening, all the onus is on us because listening

is a gift to others. These individuals want to talk to us because they value us and view us with such regard that they are willing to share. The least we can do is to be present in the moment and listen.

Know the canvas, know the questions, and know that you have the ability to add the first beautiful brushstrokes of listening within this process of creating amazing vocal art. With attentive ears, we are able to add depth and character to our creation with the vivid and wide-ranging colors of our next skill, the colors of sharing.

ART of the CONVERSATION — *Big Takeaways & Next Steps*

CHAPTER FIVE

Sharing Your Colors

Most definitions of communication allude to the idea that it is a "mutual sharing or exchange of ideas between a group of at least two people." Mutual, as in, there is no such thing as a one-sided conversation. Sure, one-sided moments exist because we all know people who love the sound of their voices. However, only one person talking is considered a monologue, and nobody likes to be on the other side of someone else's monologue unless while watching a play. The point is, by definition, that a genuine conversation cannot exist unless at least two parties are sharing. ✱

For most people, sharing comes more naturally than listening. People like to talk—mostly about themselves or about things they feel are important. Lately sharing seems to have turned more generic and manufactured. Forms, such as social media and the "like" button, constantly tempt us to share what we think people want to hear, in exactly the way they want to hear it. We repost things with which we want to be associated, and sharing has become more communal than personal. In turn, we become mundane and boxed in. Forget nuance; there is no room or time for that. If I see something that expresses how I feel, I reshare it. With the click of a button, I can adopt a hive mindset, declare my tribe, and excuse myself from the vulnerability of sharing my authentic, true self—and creating my own art. I am absolved from the challenge of working through the process. This is a "paint by number" approach in its most unfortunate form. The fear is that the world might not like something original I present, but I know it will like this other "viral" thing. In the artistic world, this approach would be called a forgery.

True conversationalists—good vocal artists—must move beyond generic, manufactured, communally-driven sharing to a more personal and meaningful approach. We have a palette of colors at our disposal, centered on the core of who we are. The shades and tones of those colors are uniquely our own. And while they may reflect our vulnerable range of the good, the bad, the known, and the "I haven't made my mind up yet," at the very least they are absolutely, admirably genuine.

The prolific leadership author and speaker Seth Godin states: "An artist is someone who uses bravery, insight, creativity, and boldness to challenge the status quo. And an artist takes it personally." Authentic sharing,
✱ the kind that leads to beautiful vocal art, expands our

52 Chapter Five | *Sharing Your Colors*

thinking to a more intentional process, instead of a passive reshare of a faded meme. Picture the baton hand-offs that happen during relay races—that brief transitional moment in time when both runners have a hand on the baton. One starts to run as the other slows to make sure the hand-off is smooth. This is called *sharing space*.

In a sharing space moment, we witness the give and take that leaves room for each individual to carry out roles. We see the culmination of all our hard work discussed in the previous chapters—to stoke our curiosity, develop our questions, and hone our skills for listening. Our vocal art begins to come alive! We add more colors and shades, and expand on our common ground with another human being. We are then poised to create the opportunity to communicate and the respect to be heard in collaboration with others.

As expected, we will likely encounter some obstacles and some opportunities that will affect this process of sharing. Amid the graceful (or initially awkward—that is ok, too!) hand-off of sharing, any number of opportunities exist. Keeping these opportunities in mind helps us remember that the goal of our exchanges is to build common ground. To accomplish this, our sharing must be personal.

SHARING OPPORTUNITY #1
We share who we are

First and foremost, we want to share authentically. We put away "prescribed" authenticity, the impulse to morph into the likeness of a desired group, to be associated with a particular movement, or to expand an assumed influence. Prescribed authenticity happens when we are not really being ourselves but a version that makes others comfortable. However, counterfeit art is not worth much; and honestly, painstakingly trying to maintain all those fake versions can be downright exhausting. Prescribed authenticity does not represent who we are; it is the cheap version.

Those artists who truly make meaningful and transformational impact are those who share their art openly, passionately, and authentically with the world. In the same way, we must paint on our canvases with *our* colors, not someone else's and especially not what we are *told* to use.

SHARING OPPORTUNITY #2
We share what we think

Second, we want to share transparently. Honestly. Sharing the thoughts that come from who we are. At this point, we want to utilize the listening skills that we have learned. You see, offering an opinion as if it were fact is very easy to do. If I speak with an overabundance of confidence, people would be less likely to question what I say. Blanket statements are easy but can also be insensitive—and can easily become weaponized.

On the other hand, listening constructively from the outset mutes our perceptions and looks for the opportunities that exist. This approach will absolutely inform our sharing. Putting better listening into practice manifests a fuller understanding of the other person. Notice I said fuller, not complete. We may never completely understand another individual, but we can gain a fuller understanding as we share and listen, allowing us to expand our knowledge about why a person may act or believe in a certain way.

This greater appreciation and fuller understanding then affects our turn to share. We now have the understanding that what we think looks very different from a diatribe of *I have something to prove.* Perhaps we may even become teachable, while most certainly more empathetic. In these moments, we can embrace the curiosity we have begun to value, confident that curiosity does not equal compromise. Staying curious means we care enough to ask good questions so we can better understand another person's point of view. In turn, we are able to share from a place of honesty *and* value another human being—things that aren't mutually exclusive!

SHARING OPPORTUNITY #3
We share what we feel

Sharing who we are and what we think inevitably connects us to our final sharing opportunity: to share what we feel. Sharing our feelings takes vulnerability. It is a brave step to say, "I feel _____ about ..." It is comparable to that moment when we reach out our baton in the hand-off and feel nervous about whether or not the other person will reach back to receive it. We cannot avoid the discomfort that extending ourselves creates. Art has always meant putting ourselves ✱ on display to a certain degree. And while it is true that we want to exercise wisdom by sharing appropriately for the relationship (the waiter probably does not need to know that you're estranged from your dad), sharing our genuine feelings opens the door for empathy, leading to truth. Feelings are naturally disarming, especially when offered from a place of authenticity. We could all use a little more truth and transparency in our lives. As Mark Twain once said, "If you tell the truth, you don't have to remember anything." Sounds like a refreshing way to live, if you ask me.

These sharing opportunities give us hope that common ground can be found and that we are able to utilize new skills at our disposal to guide us on our way. Now, are any of these opportunities giving you pause? Do they sound implausible or, perhaps, too naive? It is true that obstacles can come between our hopeful willingness to genuinely share, especially in our current, less engaged reality. One option is to accept that as fact, as insurmountable odds that keep us stuck, brush in hand, staring at an unfinished work.

Having said that, does anyone actually enjoy standing around watching paint dry?! Instead of accepting a deadlocked fate of "artist's block," we can give names to obstacles we encounter in our quest to create vocal art. Once named, these obstacles can be worked through and explored, allowing us to keep moving forward on our journey and become better, more effective artists (and humans) in the process.

SHARING OBSTACLE #1
Internal unsettledness

* Sometimes the canvas on which we work looks much

like a mirror. Sometimes we must take a long, hard look into it, and then face what looks back at us. Our initial obstacle to sharing challenges us to do this very thing. Internal unsettledness is the first obstacle to genuine, common-ground-building sharing. Perhaps something in us is not settled in one or more of the three opportunity areas. Sharing who we are, what we think, or what we feel would be incredibly difficult if the prospect of any one of those fills us with dread. Now is the time when we must ask a few curious questions of ourselves: Is there something internal that is getting in the way because we will not deal with some discomfort that lives within? Is there something within us we are avoiding?

Only we can answer those questions genuinely, and only we can know if we are ready to deal with the answers. However, may I make a suggestion? You have already shown a great deal of bravery by picking up this book, by reading through the ideas, and by being willing to consider you may have something to learn about the way you communicate. Whatever internal unsettledness that might exist to derail your progress, I would venture to guess you are brave enough to take whatever next step is necessary to face it. You have everything to gain and some beautiful artwork to create in the process.

SHARING OBSTACLE #2
Too much noise

Are you ever in the mood to turn down the volume of the world a few levels or maybe even mute the world entirely? The idiom, "Stop the world; I want to get off," comes to mind. Many days, sharing can feel difficult because too much noise is going on around us, whether internal or external.

There are times when we intentionally create excessive noise in the world because we do not want to deal with what comes up internally when we sit in the quiet. (Sound familiar? Yeah, obstacle #1 is not going away, my friend.) Ever notice sometimes the louder someone's life is externally, the more unsettled they might be internally? If we are to successfully take advantage of the opportunities for sharing our colors, we have to slow down to be quiet enough to discover who we are, what we think, and what we feel. Remember, sharing is a personal endeavor; it is not prescriptive and cannot be divorced from our individual investment in its success.

The noise around us comes from within as well as from without. In our world today, we experience an abundance of debating. We see it, hear it, and take part in it (more often online than in person; any surprises there?). We may want to prove to people that we are right/knowledgeable/know what is going on. We avoid showing any weakness or, heaven forbid, appearing teachable. It is a scenario of "I am more right because I know more than you do" vs talking about what is actually going on. Debating is not personal; debates are about who is right, not what is right. ==If our goal in sharing is to win a debate, we ultimately lose.== The goal is to build common ground, not more pillars. If our goal is building relationships/common ground then the skills we have been discussing are the ones we are going to need. If your goal is to win a debate, you probably need a different book.

With noise obstacles, we must pay attention to what is within our control. We can work on the chaos inside us; and while we may not be able to control what is happening in the world, we are able to take some ownership over our exposure to that external noise. Avoiding the triggers of social media or exercising boundaries can keep the volume at an appropriate level. We are also able to exert some measure of control over the person who shows up to communicate (i.e. you and I). We can learn that sharing and talking are not necessarily the same thing. It's possible to talk a long time and not actually share anything. That is what my life used to be. I want better for you.

SHARING OBSTACLE #3
Weak relationships

When we have become settled within ourselves and have quieted the noise, we can still face obstacles when we are sharing within a fragile relationship. Relationships inevitably go through certain milestones where emotional equity is built. This does not mean you cannot share with a person you do not know very well. It does mean that it is important to have an awareness of the relationship status—so that if we find ourselves holding back, we can understand why that might be. Strangely enough, often it is not strangers or mere acquaintances who give us pause with sharing.

Sometimes we find ourselves holding back within relationships where we assume we are our strongest. What appears to be a tight-knit relationship might actually be built on something very small and fragile—because it has never been tested. It is much easier to share with someone with whom we have overcome conflict, walked through difficult times together, and come out the other side. Perhaps at one point this was a strong connection, but it has gone through inevitable changes as relationships do. Realizing this can be a scary proposition.

Personally, I find this type of situation to be more of an "opportunity in disguise," in many ways, than an obstacle. As soon as we recognize that we are not sharing within a relationship we deemed close, we gain the ability to take a different approach. We can reinvest in the relational equity with that person—or we can also reconcile that something has changed—and decide not to. Either way, we will approach our sharing with more openness and significantly more intentionality. Whether the relationship continues or not, we will have found a path forward.

ART of the CONVERSATION
Big Takeaways & Next Steps

CHAPTER SIX

Your Studio, Your Legacy

I am going to teach you a new word. Well, odds are it will be a new word to you. And even if you already know this term, I think you will agree that it's a good one. It is the kind of word that you can casually use in a sentence at parties if you are looking to impress someone.

The word is *oeuvre* (pronounced "[URV] + [RUH]"), or if you are into phonetic pronunciations: œ-vruh.

Great word, right?! Not only is it great because it rolls off the tongue in a satisfyingly smooth manner but also the definition of oeuvre masterfully pulls together the central theme of this vocal art journey. An oeuvre is defined by the Merriam-Webster dictionary as, "a substantial body of work constituting the lifework of a writer, an artist, or a composer." It is the work of an ✶ artist regarded collectively.

You did not even know when you started this book, that you, my friend, have an oeuvre. We all do. We have a collection of works—vocal artwork—that exists in our personal studios. These oeuvres confirm our role as artists, display the facets of our curiosity, and encompass our connections with others. Perhaps even more importantly, our collected works represent all phases of our processes, not just the items that fill us with confidence. It is an important distinction. Perhaps it would be easier to think about our vocal art as a curated showing of all the pieces for which we are most proud. Instead, let us think of our vocal art as on display in an artist's studio, rather than an exhibition—less edited, more honest.

Years ago, a friend of mine visited the Academia Gallery in Florence, Italy where Michaelangelo's David is housed. David is, without doubt, an impressive feat of creativity. Yet, for all its marbled magnificence, David was not the work that left the biggest impression on my friend. While the majority of visitors naturally flocked to David, off to the side, in a much smaller room, my friend found fascination in a collection of Michaelangelo's unfinished works—large slabs of stone, blocky and rough with just the initial suggestions of a hand, arm, or face emerging from them. These were not the polished final products typically appropriate for the gallery, but the genuineness of their forms was what captivated my friend. ==It was the knowledge that even a master such as== ✱ ==Michaelangelo had a process, had to go through the effort, revisions, and maybe even make mistakes along the way.==

We have covered much information in this book; and

since you are still here, I want you to know your dedication to creating communication that is meaningful, authentic, and potentially very different from your norm is commendable. Perhaps also a little daunting. Please know that this book does not offer a "one and done" formula.

Typically speaking, as human beings, we cannot flip a switch to immediately experience wholesale change from old habits. However, remember that we are artists who are honing a craft, building our skills over time to create vocal artwork that, in our everyday lives, will enhance our communication and connection with others. True artists put their mastery to the test, not only enjoying the finished work but also welcoming the lessons that come from the endeavor as well.

As we prepare to take our artist's kit out of the studio and into the world, putting into practice all that we have discussed, I want to leave you with these last few big picture ideas. Keep these things in mind throughout the process of compiling your greater body of work—your oeuvre:

BIG PICTURE IDEA #1
Maintain a vision for your art

Pack up your canvas, prime your curiosity, include all the brushes and colors that you now know you own, and decide for yourself whether or not this is a journey worth taking. Once we have adopted the premise that we can create vocal art and that the byproduct of this process is greater connection, that belief keeps us motivated to walk out the necessary steps. What kind of relationships do you want to have? Whom do you want to show up as when you are engaging with others?

Revisit the ideas in the earlier chapters of this book and use the reference included at the end of this book to remind yourself of the opportunities that await you and to be prepared for the obstacles you may encounter. I can promise there will be ample reasons for us to be discouraged during our creative process. Yet, we do not have to allow those reasons to deter us. We can maintain a vision (dare I say, hope) for what our art can look like. We can prepare ourselves and ultimately bring our vocal art to fruition.

BIG PICTURE IDEA #2
Art is sensitive to temperature

We know now that our vocal art has value; therefore, we must take good care of it. We would not leave a valuable piece of art in a hot car in summer or sitting out in the rain, and then hope for the best. In the same way, we must treat our vocal art with appropriate attention. To steward our gift well, we must be willing to do what needs to be done to keep it in the best condition. This includes facing head-on any of those areas that challenged us in the earlier chapters. Perhaps we realize we cannot move forward with our art because we have had too many perceptions clouding our ability to listen? Maybe we have become aware of how internally unsettled we currently are and that we cannot share genuinely until we deal with this hurdle?

Now is when we get to decide to be brave and vulnerable, taking some personal growth steps that can adjust the temperature to a more optimal setting for our artwork to remain in beautiful condition.

BIG PICTURE IDEA #3
Good art stands the test of time

At the end of the day, we want to know that all our efforts and our embrace of this process amounts to something. We want to know that it all makes a difference. Good art stands the test of time. Again and again, over decades and centuries, it speaks to people. In a universal way, visual art connects people; and vocal art has the power to do the same—and beyond. Once again, Seth Godin brings this thought to mind: "Art is a personal gift that changes the recipient. An artist is an individual who creates art. The more people you change, the more you change them, the more effective your art is." ✶

There are so many ways we can choose to spend our time: endless distractions, the temptation to be in a hurry, or focused inside our own little bubble. Instead, pop that bubble, turn the focus outward, and create the art of conversation with the people around us so great change can happen. Every new conversation is a chance for a new connection. By creating space to meet universal human desires, we offer an opportunity for communication and for respect to be heard.

Once again, there is beauty in the world.

So go create your art!

Big Takeaways & Next Steps

REFERENCE
Vocal Art Key Takeaways

ART of the
CONVERSATION

💬 All human beings desire **the opportunity to communicate and the respect to be heard.**

💬 Every person is an artist in the sense that the conversations we have create **vocal art.**

Curiosity is the canvas—the foundation—for all of your vocal art, and curiosity...

👎 is not compromising our convictions.   👍 is courageous.

👎 does not have to mean conflict.   👍 produces connection.

👎 does not equal complaining.   👍 is contagious

5 Techniques for Underpainting

① Ask what/how questions rather than why questions.

② Ask a follow-up question before making a statement.

③ Ask for an invitation before giving your opinion.

④ Understand the relationship.

⑤ Consider the context.

Your Legacy, Your Oeuvre

Maintain a vision for your art.

Art is sensitive to temperature.

Good art stands the test of time.

Brushstrokes of Listening

OBSTACLES

Perceived understanding: "I already know that."

Perceived outcomes: "I already know what will happen."

Perceived reaction: "I already know what I will feel—and I will not like it."

OPPORTUNITIES

Give undivided attention.

Listen for perspective before giving your perception.

Show empathy.

Use candor; embrace boundaries.

Sharing Your Colors

OBSTACLES

Internal unsettledness.

Too much noise.

Weak relationships.

OPPORTUNITIES

Share who we are.

Share what we think.

Share what we feel.

A Time for Gratitude

If I had to express my gratitude and appreciation for everyone who invited me to speak on *Art of the Conversation*, believed in this project, encouraged me along the way, and helped shape and publish this book, it would be another book. There is no such thing as a "self-made" person. Everyone has someone whose shoulders they stand on, arms they hold, and feet they follow. I am no different. I will attempt to show my gratitude and say thank you to as many of these people as I can, recognizing my own limitations in that I cannot thank all of you by name. Whether your name is mentioned or not, you know who you are and the impact you have had on me, *Art of the Conversation*, and this book project. So to you all—THANK YOU!

I want to express deep gratitude to all the companies, organizations, and conferences who have invited me to share *Art of the Conversation* with their teams and audiences since 2016. In the early stages of this project, a few people took the risk of giving me the mic, which gave *Art of the Conversation* the credibility to be taught nationally and internationally. So to Todd, Tami, Ryan, Traci, and Barry, and Nika—THANK YOU for believing in me and *Art of the Conversation*. To those other companies and conferences, thank you for being a part of the journey and inviting me to guide your people to becoming remarkable vocal artists.

To the amazing folks who helped me get all of this content into a book, THANK YOU. For the hours of transcribing, editing, formatting, and so much more, I will forever be grateful. Each one of you played a vital role that has allowed this project to come to life. Because of your work, thousands (and hopefully millions) of people will become great vocal artists. Erin, April, Annie, and Wendy: I am grateful for your time, belief, and work. I could not have done it without you.

Oh Nathan! I think outside of my family, you have heard my voice more than any other person. You have also heard *Art of the Conversation* more than anyone in the world. Thank you, my friend, for believing in me from the start of this journey. For the countless hours of recording video and audio, editing, posting, brainstorming, and listening to and trying every idea with me, thank you just does not seem enough. In addition to all of this, our conversations around life, beliefs, mindset, and business have helped shape me and how I live in this crazy world. The best is yet to come for both of us, and I am grateful to be on this path with you.

Hey Mom and Dad—I wrote a book! There is not enough time here to express my gratitude to you both. From struggling to speak to speaking for a living, you always encouraged, challenged, and took the risks with me. You cared for and invested in me to pursue so many ideas, hobbies, possible career paths, and just random "I think this could work" concepts; and you were always there by my side in success or failure. I cannot describe my thankfulness. Just know I am not where I am today and this book is not possible without you!

To my three boys—I mainly wrote this book for you. Taking nothing for granted, I wanted to give you a piece of me that will outlive me. You have seen and will continue to see that becoming a remarkable vocal artist is a never-ending journey even for your Dad. You have seen me making my best artwork and you have seen me make my worst artwork. Thank you for being along for the ride. I hope this book serves you in your future.

To my best friend—I love you! Jessica, you have stood by me for more than 20 years. You have encouraged and supported every opportunity to present, speak, travel, and share *Art of the Conversation*. You are supernaturally kind, forgiving, loving, and caring. Everyone in your sphere knows this and is changed because they have been with you. My name may be on the cover, yet your spirit is on every page. Words fall short for me when it comes to you. You leave me speechless. So I will say THANK YOU and attempt to demonstrate my gratitude for who you are every day.

In conclusion, I must say thank you and show gratitude to the ONE who answered well. Thank you for demonstrating that everyone is worthy of a conversation. No matter a person's stage and standing in life, nationality or race, friend or enemy, similar beliefs or polar opposite beliefs, if they look like you or if they don't, if it was accepted to engage a person or not, and so much more; YOU lived a life defined by being approachable, conversational, and sacrificial. Thank you for giving me permission to be as bold in my conversations and interactions as you were. May I, and everyone who reads and implements this book into their life, be known for answering well too.

About the Author

Jonathan R. Parker is a distinguished leader, influential strategist, and captivating communicator with over 15 years of professional speaking and leadership experience. Jonathan is dedicated to empowering executives to elevate their self-awareness, emotional intelligence, and communication proficiency, thereby transforming their teams and companies.

Known for delivering impactful keynotes, facilitating engaging workshops, and conducting bespoke corporate training sessions, Jonathan has graced prestigious stages across the United States and spoken to audiences nationally and internationally, including a memorable appearance at TEDx. As a certified *5 Voices* guide through GiANT Worldwide, and having completed an esteemed leadership coaching program in Predictive Leadership Behaviors and Life Intensive with GiANT London, Jonathan brings a wealth of expertise to the table.

Jonathan is married to his best friend, Jessica, and they have three strong, energetic, and talented boys.

Connect with him @thejonathanrparker.com.

Made in the USA
Middletown, DE
09 February 2025